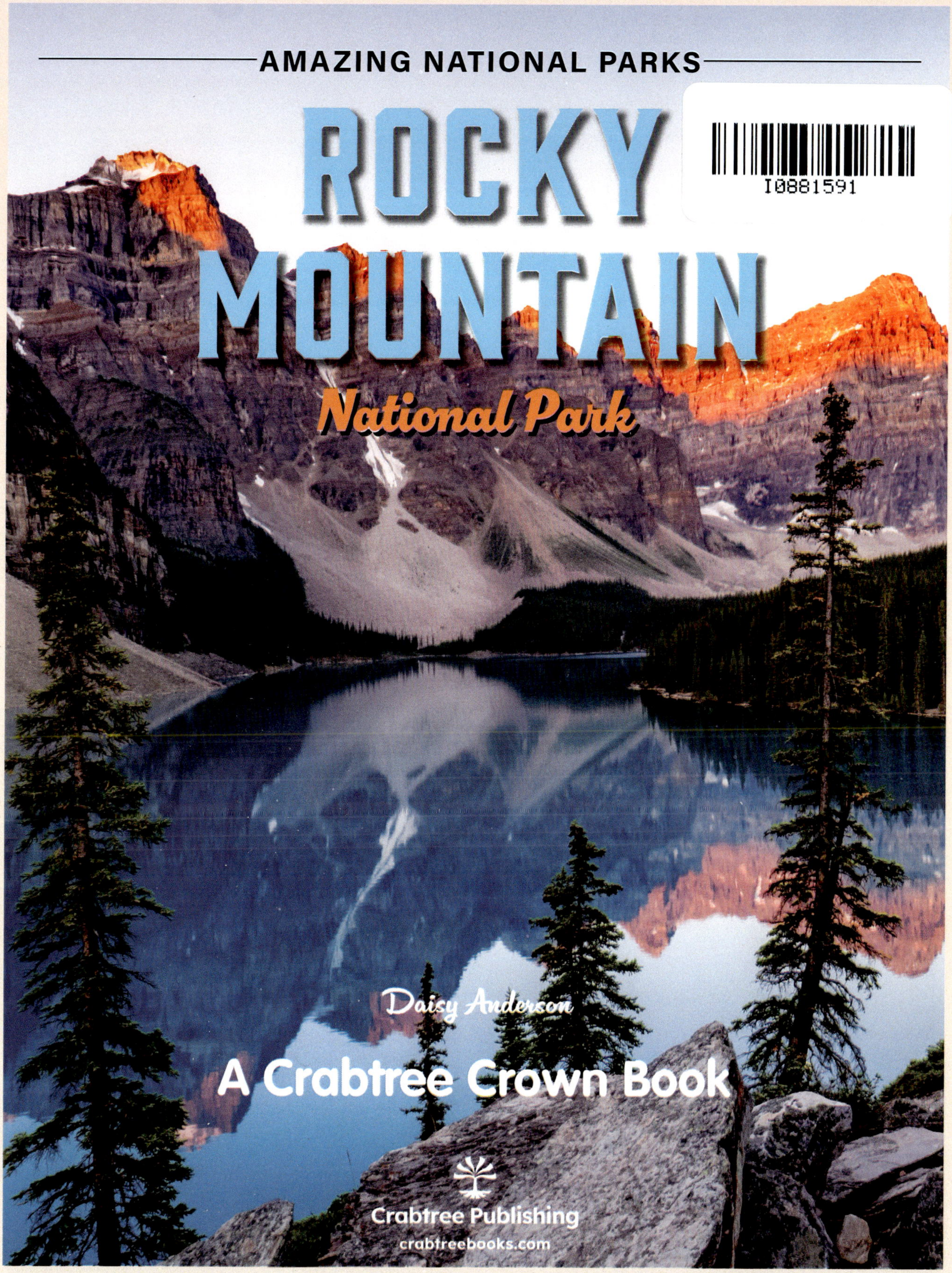
AMAZING NATIONAL PARKS
ROCKY MOUNTAIN
National Park
Daisy Anderson
A Crabtree Crown Book
Crabtree Publishing
crabtreebooks.com

# School-to-Home Support for Caregivers and Teachers

This appealing book is designed to teach students about core subject areas. Students will build upon what they already know about the subject, and engage in topics that they want to learn more about. Here are a few guiding questions to help readers build their comprehension skills. Possible answers appear here in red.

## Before Reading:

*What do I know about Rocky Mountain National Park?*

- *I know the national park is in the Rocky Mountains.*
- *I know many people visit Rocky Mountain National Park.*

*What do I want to learn about this topic?*

- *I want to learn what people can see in the national park.*
- *I want to learn what people can do in the national park.*

## During Reading:

*I'm curious to know...*

- *I'm curious to know what kinds of animals live in the national park.*
- *I'm curious to know about the mountains in the national park.*

*How is this like something I already know?*

- *I know that mountain lions live in the mountains.*
- *I know that the Rocky Mountains are the largest mountain range in North America.*

## After Reading:

*What was the author trying to teach me?*

- *The author was trying to teach me about why so many people visit Rocky Mountain National Park.*
- *The author was trying to teach me what visitors can see at the national park.*

*How did the photographs and captions help me understand more?*

- *The photographs helped me picture what the national park looks like.*
- *The captions gave me extra information about what there is to see at the national park.*

# TABLE OF CONTENTS

**Chapter 1**
Welcome to Rocky Mountain National Park . . . . . . . . . . . . . . . . . . . . . . 4

**Chapter 2**
The Land and Climate . . . . . . . . . . . . . . . . . . 10

**Chapter 3**
Plants in the Park . . . . . . . . . . . . . . . . . . . . . 14

**Chapter 4**
Animals in the Park . . . . . . . . . . . . . . . . . . . . 18

**Chapter 5**
Tips on What to See . . . . . . . . . . . . . . . . . . . . 22

**Chapter 6**
Tips on What to Do . . . . . . . . . . . . . . . . . . . . . 26

**Glossary** . . . . . . . . . . . . . . . . . . . . . . . . . . . . 30

**Index** . . . . . . . . . . . . . . . . . . . . . . . . . . . . . . . . 31

**Comprehension Questions** . . . . . . . . . . . . . . . . 31

**About the Author** . . . . . . . . . . . . . . . . . . . . . . . 32

## Chapter 1

# WELCOME TO ROCKY MOUNTAIN NATIONAL PARK

Snow-covered mountain peaks rise against blue skies. These mountains are home to one of the highest national parks in the United States. Millions of people come to Rocky Mountain National Park every year!

### Know the Park

The U.S. government owns national parks and takes care of them. National parks are used to help protect natural areas.

## Know the Park

The Continental Divide is a mountain ridge that runs through the Rocky Mountains and the national park. Water on the divide's west side drains into the Pacific Ocean. Water on the east side runs into the Atlantic Ocean.

Rocky Mountain National Park is in Colorado. It covers 415 square miles (1,075 square kilometers) of the Rocky Mountains. The national park is a small part of the Rocky Mountains. The entire mountain range stretches from Alaska to Mexico.

# BEFORE IT WAS A PARK

For thousands of years, Native American peoples such as the Ute and Arapaho spent warm seasons in the area where the park is today. **Traders** from Europe carried goods through the mountains in the early 1800s. Miners searched for gold in the area in the mid-1800s. As more people **settled** there, the Ute and Arapaho peoples were pushed off their lands.

### Know the Park

Some of the trails made by the Ute and Arapaho peoples are still used as trails in the national park today.

In the late 1800s, the beautiful Rocky Mountains began to attract visitors from all over the United States. People in the Colorado towns around the mountains wanted to create a protected area.

# FOUNDING THE PARK

Many in Colorado worked to help create the national park. People gave talks about it and wrote letters to the government about why they wanted a national park in the area. On January 26, 1915, President Woodrow Wilson signed the Rocky Mountain National Park Act.

Mary Belle King Sherman

### Know the Park

Mary Belle King Sherman is called the "National Park Lady" because she gave many talks about why Rocky Mountain National Park should be formed. She also worked to build support for six more national parks.

## THE PARK TODAY

Rocky Mountain National Park is the 26th-largest national park in the United States. It has some of the highest peaks in the Rocky Mountains. More than 4.5 million people enjoy Rocky Mountain National Park every year!

## Chapter 2
# THE LAND AND CLIMATE

The rocks that make up the Rocky Mountains formed 1.7 billion years ago. The area was once covered by seawater. The rock was **uplifted** into mountains about 75 million years ago.

**Glaciers** have shaped the mountains over the last 300,000 years. Huge amounts of slow-moving ice and snow created wide, U-shaped valleys. Moving glaciers also created **moraines** when they left behind rock and soil.

### Know the Park

Today the national park has eight small glaciers. It also has about 22 year-round snow and ice patches.

*All of the national park's small glaciers are found in bowl-shaped areas at the head, or upper part, of mountain valleys.*

## CLIMATE

The national park has three **climate** regions based on **elevation**. The area below 9,000 feet (2,743 meters) is called montane. The subalpine region is found between 9,000 and 11,000 feet (2,743 and 3,353 meters). Alpine tundra is at the very top, above 11,000 feet (3,353 meters).

*Bierstadt Lake is a subalpine lake.*

The national park has warm summers and cold winters. It's always colder at the top of the mountains than at the bottom. It might be 56 °F (13 °C) in the alpine tundra but 70 °F (21 °C) in the montane at the same time. Summers often have afternoon thunderstorms. Winters bring snow, especially high on the mountains.

## Chapter 3

# PLANTS IN THE PARK

Different plants grow at different elevations in the national park. More than 100 **species** of grasses blanket meadows in the montane. Forests of fir, aspen, and pine trees cover this region's **slopes**. Willows and water birch trees grow along streams or next to lakes.

### Know the Park

Quaking aspen trees have smooth, white bark. Their leaves turn golden yellow in the fall. They're called quaking aspen because their leaves shake in the breeze, making it look like the whole tree is quaking, or trembling.

*Evergreen trees keep their needles and stay green all year.*

Evergreen trees such as fir, spruce, and pine cover the mountainside in the subalpine region. They grow tall in forests on the lower slopes. But the weather is colder and the wind blows harder higher up in the mountains. There, trees grow slowly and are shorter.

Trees can't live in the cold and wind of the alpine tundra. Only grasses, mosses, and other plants that are low to the ground grow in these highest areas of the national park.

**Know the Park**

About one-third of the national park is alpine tundra. The national park is one of the few places in the U.S. where you can see alpine tundra by car.

# FLOWERING PLANTS

Wildflowers color the national park in the spring and summer. Blanketflowers bloom in montane meadows. The columbine, Colorado's state flower, grows in both montane and subalpine forests. Even the alpine tundra has tiny flowers, such as forget-me-nots.

*Blanketflowers bloom from mid-June to late August.*

# Chapter 4
# ANIMALS IN THE PARK

Rocky Mountain National Park is full of wildlife. Mountain lions are the national park's largest **predator**. They hunt mule deer and elk. Ten kinds of squirrels scamper through the trees. Hawks, owls, and more than 270 other species of birds have been spotted in the area. The national park also has more than 140 kinds of butterflies.

*Black-billed magpies sometimes eat ticks off the backs of deer, elk, and moose.*

## BIGHORN SHEEP

Bighorn sheep are the national park's **symbol**. Between 300 to 400 live there. Males may weigh more than 300 pounds (136 kilograms). Bighorn sheep's hooves are split to pinch and grip rock as they climb and jump.

# PIKAS

Pikas may look like hamsters, but they're related to rabbits. Pikas live in the alpine tundra. They collect plants for the winter and store them in piles called haystacks. Pikas are noisy. They call and sing to warn each other of danger, protect their territory, and find mates.

# WATCHING WILDLIFE

The national park has herds of elk and other large animals such as moose. It's important to remember that all the animals are wild. Keeping your distance and watching through binoculars or by zooming in with your camera is the safest way to enjoy the wildlife.

*Visitors should keep at least two bus-lengths away from wildlife.*

# Chapter 5
# TIPS ON WHAT TO SEE

### Know the Park

Climbing Longs Peak is not a hike. It takes special equipment and mountain climbing experience to make it to the top.

## LONGS PEAK

Longs Peak is the tallest peak in the national park at 14,259 feet (4,346 meters). Its flat top can be seen from almost everywhere in the park. Thousands of mountain climbers try to reach the top every summer.

**Know the Park**

Many Parks Curve is a stop along Trail Ridge Road. Cars can park there for a view of meadows, Longs Peak, and Deer Mountain.

## TRAIL RIDGE ROAD

Trail Ridge Road is the highest paved road in any U.S. national park. It runs for 48 miles (77 kilometers) between Rocky Mountain National Park's east and west sides. Cars climb through evergreen forests up to the alpine tundra at 12,183 feet (3,713 meters) and then head back down.

*Alpine Visitor Center is only open during the summer season.*

## ALPINE VISITOR CENTER

Alpine Visitor Center is the highest visitor center of all the national parks in the United States. It's 11,796 feet (3,595 meters) high in the mountains and has amazing views. A short but steep trail near the visitor center goes through part of the alpine tundra.

# BEAR LAKE

Bear Lake is one of the most visited areas in the national park. A free shuttle bus takes people to the lake and its trails. The Bear Lake Loop is a trail for all ages and is wheelchair friendly. Another trail leads to the Alberta Falls waterfall.

*Bear Lake is one of the most photographed places in the park.*

# Chapter 6
# TIPS ON WHAT TO DO

### Know the Park

Visitors to the national park should follow the Leave No Trace Principles. They include staying on trails, leaving no trash behind, and treating wildlife with respect.

## HIKING

Rocky Mountain National Park has 355 miles (571 kilometers) of hiking trails. Hikes range from easy walks around lakes to steep climbs in the mountains that may take days. The national park also has 26 picnic areas.

### Know the Park

The higher the elevation at Rocky Mountain National Park, the harder it is to breathe. This is because the air is thinner at higher elevations. Visitors to the national park should always be aware of their surroundings and return to lower elevations if they start to feel unwell. It's also important to drink plenty of water.

## CAMPING

The national park has five campgrounds. The largest has 244 campsites. Hikers may also camp at wilderness campsites throughout the national park.

# FISHING

The national park has many places to fish. It has 450 miles (724 kilometers) of rivers and streams and 147 lakes. The Colorado River begins there. Four kinds of trout can be caught in these waters.

Whether you camp, hike, or just drive in for the day, Rocky Mountain National Park is a mountain adventure!

# GLOSSARY

**climate** (KLYE-mit): The usual weather conditions of a place over a long period of time

**elevation** (el-uh-VAY-shun): The height of a place above sea level

**glaciers** (GLAY-shurz): Giant masses of ice and snow that move like very slow rivers

**moraines** (muh-REYNZ): Piles of soil and rock left behind by a moving glacier

**predator** (PRED-uh-tur): An animal that hunts other animals for food

**settled** (SET-ld): Moved to a new place and made it a home

**slopes** (SLOHPS): Ground that slants upward or downward

**species** (SPEE-seez): A group of animals or plants that are similar and can reproduce with one another

**symbol** (SIM-buhl): An object or a design that stands for something else

**traders** (TREY-derz): People who buy, sell, or exchange goods

**uplift** (UHP-lift): An increase in the vertical elevation of Earth's surface as a result of natural causes

# INDEX


Alpine Visitor Center 24
Bear Lake 25
bighorn sheep 19
camping 27
fishing 28
flowering plants 17
hiking 26
Longs Peak 22, 23
pikas 20
Trail Ridge Road 23


# COMPREHENSION QUESTIONS

1. Rocky Mountain National Park is in ____.
   a. Colorado
   b. Utah
   c. California
2. Trees can't live in the ____.
   a. montane
   b. subalpine
   c. alpine tundra
3. The Alpine Visitor Center is the ____ visitor center of all the national parks.
   a. largest
   b. highest
   c. smallest
4. True or False: The bald eagle is the symbol of the national park.
5. True or False: Longs Peak is the highest mountain in the national park.

**Answers:** 1. A, 2. C, 3. B, 4. False, 5. True

# ABOUT THE AUTHOR

**Daisy Anderson** loves to write real-life books for curious kids. She lives in the Midwest, where she enjoys exploring the great outdoors with her two dogs. When Daisy isn't writing, she's out hiking and having fun in nature.

Written by: Daisy Anderson
Designed by: Bobbie Houser
Series Development: James Earley
Proofreader: Melissa Boyce
Educational Consultant: Marie Lemke M.Ed.
Production manager: Candice Campbell

Photographs:
t = Top, c = Center, b = Bottom, l = Left, r = Right
Alamy: Science History Images: p. 6; Hum Images: p. 7;
Courtesy of the Women's History and Resource Center of the General Federation of Women's Clubs: p. 8
Shutterstock: Veronique Duplain: cover, p. 1; Sean Xu: p. 4, 5 t; Globe Turner: p. 5 b; Margaret.Wiktor: p. 9, 26, 29; LukeChapman: p. 10-11; Kelly vanDellen: p. 12; John Couture: p. 13; Kristi Blokhin: p. 14; Jenny CC Carter: p. 15; Stephen Moehle: p. 16; DanaForeman: p. 17; Morgan. clairew: p. 18 tl; Max Allen: p. 18 r; Georgia Evans: p. 18 bl; Perry McLeod: p. 19; M. Leonard Photography: p. 20; Jennifer McCallum: p. 21; Chris M Long: p. 22; Brian Wolski: p. 23; Kit Leong: p. 24; cvm: p. 25; Mr.Denzilla: p. 27; Scott K Baker: p. 28

**Crabtree Publishing**

**crabtreebooks.com 800-387-7650**

Printed in the U.S.A./CP2025

**Published in Canada**
**Crabtree Publishing**
616 Welland Ave.
St. Catharines, Ontario
L2M 5V6

**Published in the United States**
**Crabtree Publishing**
347 Fifth Ave
Suite 1402-145
New York, NY 10016

**Library and Archives Canada Cataloguing in Publication**
Available at Library and Archives Canada

**Library of Congress Cataloging-in-Publication Data**
Available at the Library of Congress

Hardcover: 978-1-0398-6485-6
Paperback: 978-1-0398-6554-9
Ebook (pdf): 978-1-0398-6623-2
Epub: 978-1-0398-6692-8